Soccer Superstar
Alex Morgan

by Jon M. Fishman

LERNER PUBLICATIONS ◆ MINNEAPOLIS

Note to Educators

Throughout this book, you'll find critical-thinking questions. These can be used to engage young readers in thinking critically about the topic and in using the text and photos to do so.

Lerner Publications Company
A division of Lerner Publishing Group, Inc.
241 First Avenue North
Minneapolis, MN 55401 USA

For reading levels and more information, look up this title at www.lernerbooks.com.

Main body text set in Helvetica Textbook Com Roman 23/49.
Typeface provided by Linotype AG.

Library of Congress Cataloging-in-Publication Data

Names: Fishman, Jon M., author.
Title: Soccer superstar Alex Morgan / by Jon M. Fishman.
Description: Minneapolis : Lerner Publications, [2020] | Series: Bumba books — sports superstars | Includes bibliographical references and index. | Audience: Age 4–7. | Audience: Grades K to 3.
Identifiers: LCCN 2018038338 (print) | LCCN 2018056951 (ebook) | ISBN 9781541556539 (eb pdf) | ISBN 9781541555631 (lb : alk. paper)
Subjects: LCSH: Morgan, Alex (Alexandra Patricia), 1989– —Juvenile literature. | Women soccer players—United States—Biography—Juvenile literature.
Classification: LCC GV942.7.M673 (ebook) | LCC GV942.7.M673 F57 2020 (print) | DDC 796.334092 [B] —dc23

LC record available at https://lccn.loc.gov/2018038338

Manufactured in the United States of America
1-46018-42935-10/19/2018

Table of Contents

Super Teammate

Alex Morgan kicks the ball.

She scores!

Alex is a soccer superstar.

Alex loved to play sports
as a kid.

She liked soccer, basketball,
and softball.

She played sports with her

two older sisters.

Alex tried to win every game.

After high school, Alex
went to college.
She played for her school's
soccer team.

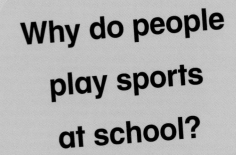

**Why do people
play sports
at school?**

Alex also played for the

United States Women's

National Team.

The team plays games

around the world.

In 2011, the team played in the Women's World Cup. Alex and her teammates finished in second place.

How can teammates help one another?

The next year, Alex and

her team played in the

Olympic Games.

They won the gold medal!

The next Women's World Cup

was in 2015.

This time, Alex helped

the United States win the

tournament.

Alex works hard to play her best.

She wants to win even more

tournaments!

Soccer Gear

jersey

cleats

shorts

soccer ball

Picture Glossary

Olympic Games

a worldwide sports contest held every four years

tournament

a series of games to decide a winner

United States Women's National Team

the top women's soccer team in the United States

Women's World Cup

a worldwide soccer contest held every four years

Read More

Derr, Aaron. *Soccer: An Introduction to Being a Good Sport.* Egremont, MA: Red Chair, 2017.

Flynn, Brendan. *Soccer Time!* Minneapolis: Lerner Publications, 2017.

Nelson, Robin. *Soccer Is Fun!* Minneapolis: Lerner Publications, 2014.

Index

Photo Credits

Image credits: Tim Warner/Getty Images, p. 5; Christof Koepsel/Getty Images, p. 6; Friedemann Vogel/Getty Images, pp. 9, 15, 23 (bottom right); Collegiate Images/Getty Images, p. 10; Ezra Shaw/Getty Images, pp. 13, 23 (bottom left); Ronald Martinez/Getty Images, pp. 17, 23 (top left); Lars Baron/FIFA/Getty Images, pp. 18, 23 (top right); David Madison/Getty Images, p. 21; karammiri/iStock/Getty Images, p. 22 (top left); CreativaImages/iStock/Getty Images, p. 22 (top right); khvost/iStock/Getty Images, p. 22 (bottom left); Dan Thornberg/EyeEm/Getty Images, p. 22 (bottom right).

Cover: Alan Smith/Icon Sportswire/Getty Images.